FERNS OF NORTHEASTERN UNITED STATES

ILLUSTRATIONS AND DESCRIPTIONS OF ALL KNOWN SPECIES
IN THE NEW ENGLAND AND MIDDLE ATLANTIC STATES

by
Farida A. Wiley

Honorary Associate in Natural Science Ed.
Department of Education, American Museum of Natural History

Illustrations by the Author, Donald D. Johnston and Suzan Swain

DOVER PUBLICATIONS, INC.
NEW YORK

Published in Canada by General Publishing Company, Ltd., 30 Lesmill Road, Don Mills, Toronto, Ontario.
Published in the United Kingdom by Constable and Company, Ltd., 10 Orange Street, London WC 2.

This Dover edition, first published in 1973, is an unabridged and corrected republication of the privately published second (1948) edition. The first edition of the work was published in 1936.

International Standard Book Number: 0-486-22946-7
Library of Congress Catalog Card Number: 73-77638

Manufactured in the United States of America
Dover Publications, Inc.
180 Varick Street
New York, N. Y. 10014

FOREWORD

THIS POCKET MANUAL ON FERNS has been written to fill the need for a book that can be conveniently carried on trips afield. Except for a few closely related forms, it is possible to recognize all of our mature ferns by outline of leaf and shape of the lower portion of the blade. The lower pinnae of all the larger ferns are shown in LIFE SIZE on the left hand page, while the drawings of the large-sized ferns have necessarily been reduced. The scale of reduction is indicated on the margin or in the text. The fronds of small ferns are shown in life size. Except for two rare ferns, the drawings have been made from specimens collected by the author, and include all known species found in New England and the Middle Atlantic States.

Ferns belong to a GROUP OF FLOWERLESS PLANTS which is a part of the PHYLUM, PTERIDOPHYTA. They, with other members of this Phylum, reproduce by means of spores, or in some instances, by buds or bulblets. The spores are produced on some portion of a leaf (frond) in minute sacs. The placement and arrangement of spore-sac groups (sori) constitute one means whereby the genera and species of ferns are determined.

When mature spores fall, and suitable conditions prevail, they develop into tiny organisms called prothallia. On the under side of each prothallium appear two kinds of reproductive organs—antheridia (male) and archegonia (female). From the union of cells from these reproductive organs there arises the asexual stage (sporophyte). This sporophyte stage in the life cycle, is the fern plant with which we are familiar and with which this book deals.

Fern stipes (stems) are stiffened by vascular bundles, consisting of thickened tissues and conducting vessels, that give support to the stipe, carry the sap, and are separated enough to form definite patterns when seen in cross section. The drawings of cross sections of stipes, shown in the text, are from cuts made one inch above the ground. These patterns of vascular bundles furnish an aid to identification. Dr. Waters, many years ago, published a key based on vascular bundle patterns in fern stipes.

Thanks are given to Mr. George T. Hastings and to Mr. and Mrs. H. A. Haring for critical reading of the first edition of "Ferns" and to Dr. Henry K. Svenson, and others for suggested changes in the text of this revised edition; and to the Brooklyn Botanic, the New York Botanical Garden, and to Mr. H. C. Merrill for granting access to their herbariums for the purpose of making comparisons.

The nomenclature has not been revised. It is that of Dr. J. K. Small's "Ferns of the Vicinity of New York", Gray's "New Manual of Botany" 7th edition, and Britton and Brown's "Illustrated Flora of the Northern States and Canada," 2nd edition. If there are variations in the scientific names given by these authors, the names are arranged in the same order as above indicated. If "Gray" and "Britton and Brown" agree, their name for the plant will only be given once.

For a list of "Varieties and Forms of Ferns of Eastern North America" see the Reprint from the American Fern Journal, Vol. 25, Pages 45–51, June 22, 1935 by C. A. Weatherby, as given under the above title.

A hand-lens of ten times (10 X) magnification will be of great assistance in the study and identification of ferns.

Since the original publication of "Ferns," the author has received innumerable requests for more information on cross section patterns found in fern stipes. To meet this need a six-page section has been added to this edition. In the original book, the patterns included only those from the base of the stipe, while in this new edition the patterns from both the top and bottom of the stipe have been included for comparative purposes. Vascular bundle patterns that are similar are shown on the same plate. The detailed descriptions of the cross section pattern will be found in the text under each species. This new material is found in no other pocket guide to ferns. Requests for raising ferns from spores, as well as ways of preserving ferns for a herbarium, have given rise to a section on these problems.

FARIDA ANNA WILEY
The American Museum of Natural History
May, 1948

CONTENTS

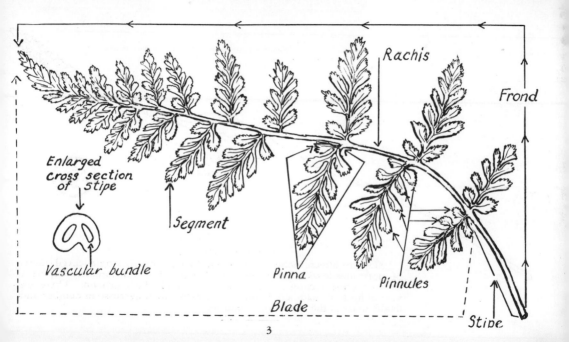

Rachis

Frond

Enlarged
cross section
of stipe

Segment

Vascular bundle

Pinna

Pinnules

Blade

Stipe

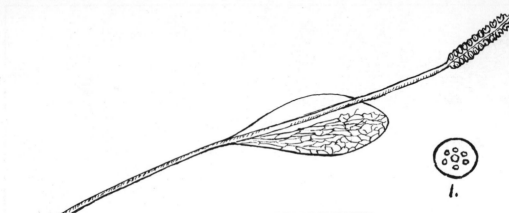

ADDER'S-TONGUE
(Ophioglossum vulgatum L.)

Two to fifteen inches long; erect; fleshy. Usually single-leaved plants of moist meadows or newly grown thickets. Fruits in summer. Figure 1 shows a cross section of stem cut about 1 inch above ground. There are several hollow chambers in the round stem which decrease in number and finally unite at the top. Not common.

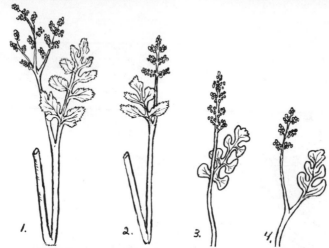

GRAPE-FERNS OR MOONWORTS (Botrychium)

1. Wood's (B. matricariaefolium A. Br.) or (B. neglectum Wood). Sterile blade lanceolate to ovate, short-stalked and pinnate. 2. Lance-leaved (B. lanceolatum (S. G. Gmel.) Ångstr.) Sterile blade sessile, triangular, finely cut. 3. Moon-fern (B. Lunaria (L.) Sw.) Sterile blade sessile, lobes crescent-shaped and often overlap. Thick in texture. 4. Hitchcock's (B. simplex E. Hitchc.) Sterile blade stalked, lobed or pinnately cut. Thick in texture. All these grow in moist woods. Numbers 1 and 2 are the most common.

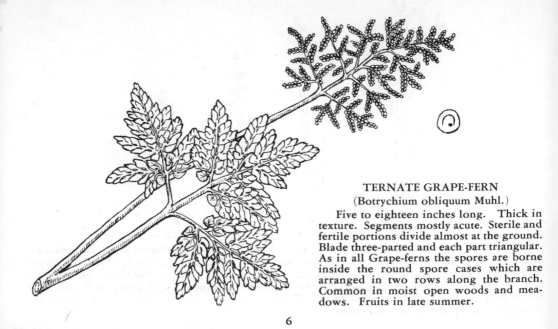

TERNATE GRAPE-FERN
(Botrychium obliquum Muhl.)

Five to eighteen inches long. Thick in texture. Segments mostly acute. Sterile and fertile portions divide almost at the ground. Blade three-parted and each part triangular. As in all Grape-ferns the spores are borne inside the round spore cases which are arranged in two rows along the branch. Common in moist open woods and meadows. Fruits in late summer.

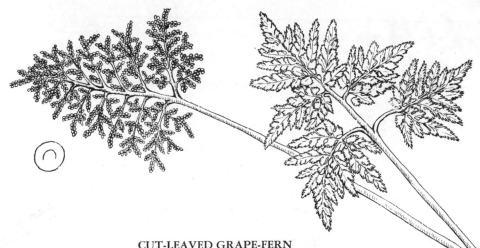

CUT-LEAVED GRAPE-FERN

(Botrychium dissectum Spreng.), or (B. obliquum var. dissectum (Spreng.) Clute)

Five to eighteen inches long. Thick in texture. Blade three-parted and each part triangular. With same texture and habitat as the Ternate Grape-fern but has the segments much more deeply cut. Fruits in late summer.

LEATHERY GRAPE-FERN
(Botrychium multifidum (S. G. Gmel.) Rupr.), or (B. silaifolium Presl.)

Five to twenty inches long. Thick in texture. Segments mostly obtuse. Three-parted, each part triangular and rather long-stalked. Sterile and fertile portions divide near the ground. In open woods and in meadows. Fruits in late summer.

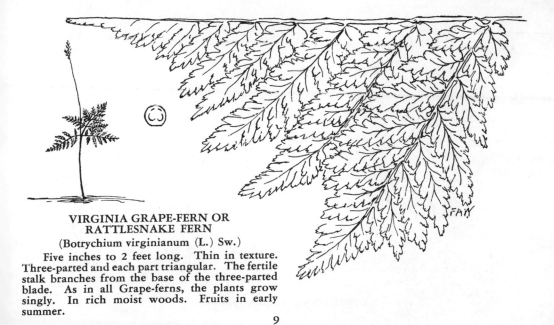

VIRGINIA GRAPE-FERN OR
RATTLESNAKE FERN
(Botrychium virginianum (L.) Sw.)

Five inches to 2 feet long. Thin in texture.
Three-parted and each part triangular. The fertile
stalk branches from the base of the three-parted
blade. As in all Grape-ferns, the plants grow
singly. In rich moist woods. Fruits in early
summer.

9

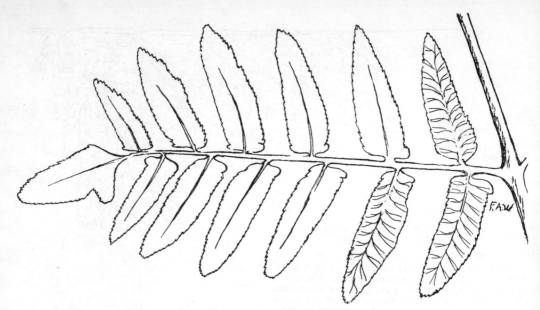

LOWER PINNA OF THE ROYAL FERN

ROYAL OR FLOWERING-FERN
(Osmunda regalis L.)

Frond shown was 33 inches long, and 12¾ inches wide at base of the blade. Sometimes twice this size. Fronds coarse in texture; erect; clustered. Page 10 shows the size and cutting of the lower Pinna. The pinnae may be almost opposite at times.

Spore cases in erect, much branched clusters at the top of the frond. Green in color, turning brown with age.

Figure 1 shows an open spore case.

Stipe and rachis are shining and free from scales. Figure 2 shows cross section of stipe. Vascular bundles brownish or light green in color. Stipe grooved.

Habitat—Edge of marshes and streams, either in open meadows or in woods.

Remarks—It is the only one of our coarse ferns which has the pinnae and pinnules so widely spaced.

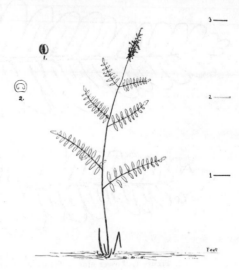

11

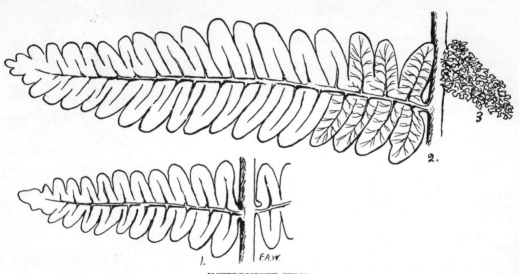

INTERRUPTED FERN
Figure 1. Lower pinna. Figure 2. Pinna from center of blade. Figure 3. A fertile pinna.

12

INTERRUPTED OR CLAYTON'S FERN
(Osmunda Claytoniana L.)

Frond shown was 46 inches long, and 11 inches broad about the center of the blade. Sometimes 5 feet or more long. Fronds coarse in texture: erect; clustered. Figure 1 on page 12 shows a sterile lower pinna. Figure 2 shows a sterile pinna just below the fruiting one. Figure 3 shows the fertile pinna. Segments rounded, almost entire and not cut to vein.

Figure 1 shows a cluster of spore cases, green when young, and brown when old. When mature they split vertically as shown in Figure 2. The number of pinnae bearing spore cases may vary but will usually develop about the center of the blade. Fruits in early spring.

Stipe and rachis covered by thick, light brown, wool-like hairs which drop off with age. The vascular bundles are golden in color and form a hooked crescent as shown in Figure 3.

Habitat—Swamps or along streams, either in open meadows or woods. Common.

Remarks—It is distinguished from the Cinnamon fern, with which it is often confused, by the more rounded pinna and segments, and the lack of the tuft of down at the base of each pinna.

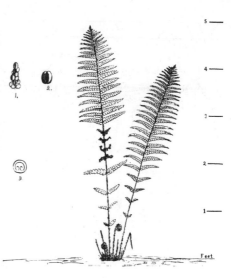

13

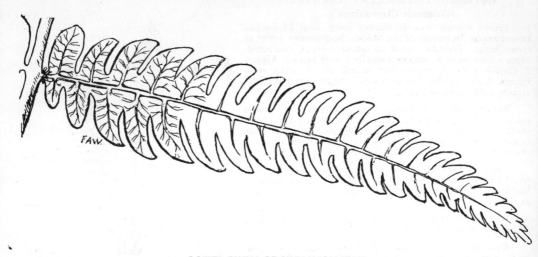

FAW.

LOWER PINNA OF CINNAMON FERN

CINNAMON FERN
(Osmunda cinnamomea L.)

Sterile frond shown was 42 inches long, and 13½ inches broad about the center of the blade. Sometimes 5 feet or more long. Fronds coarse in texture; erect; clustered. Page 14 shows the lower pinna of the sterile frond. There is a tuft of down at the base of each pinna. Segments of sterile frond somewhat pointed and cut almost to the vein.

Fertile frond very unlike sterile. All pinnae bear spore cases on the much contracted segments as shown in Figure 1. Fruits in early spring.

Stipe and rachis covered by thick, light brown, wool-like hairs which drop off with age. Figure 2 shows a cross section of the stipe. The vascular bundles are golden in color and form a hooked crescent.

Habitat—Swamps or along streams, either in open meadows or woods. Common.

Remarks—The more pointed pinnae and segments, and the tuft of down at the base of the pinna will serve to distinguish it from the Interrupted fern, with which it is often confused. Plants are sometimes found which have fronds intermediate between the sterile and fertile forms.

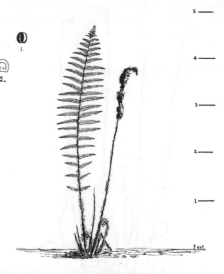

15

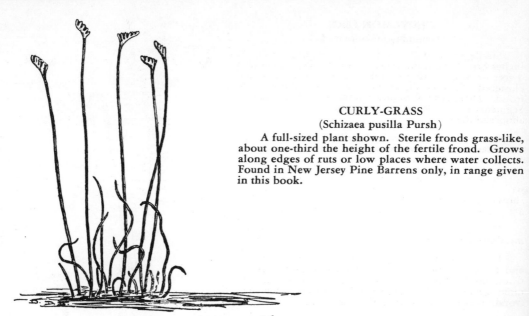

CURLY-GRASS
(Schizaea pusilla Pursh)

A full-sized plant shown. Sterile fronds grass-like, about one-third the height of the fertile frond. Grows along edges of ruts or low places where water collects. Found in New Jersey Pine Barrens only, in range given in this book.

CLIMBING OR HARTFORD FERN
(Lygodium palmatum (Bernh.) Sw.)

Frond shown reduced about half. Sometimes 4 feet long. Winds about any available prop. The small upper pinnae bear the spore cases in regularly imbricated series as shown in the upper left hand corner. Very local and rare. Wet situations.

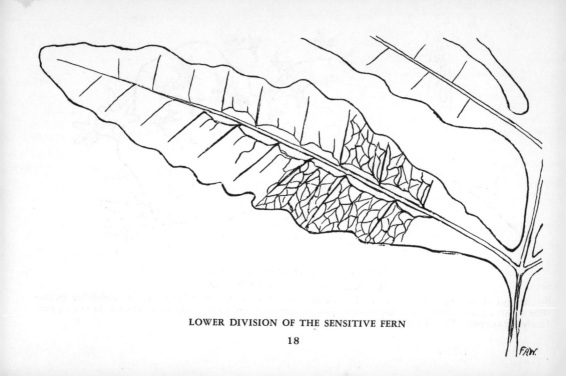

LOWER DIVISION OF THE SENSITIVE FERN

18

SENSITIVE FERN
(Onoclea sensibilis L.)

Sterile frond shown was 21 inches long and 11 inches broad at the widest point of the blade. Sometimes 3 feet long. Fronds erect; single. Coarse looking but thin in texture. Page 18 shows the lower portion of a sterile blade which is not cut entirely to the midvein. The divisions are sometimes almost entire and sometimes deeply cut. The veins are curved and joined, others form a chain-like network along the midvein.

Fertile frond very unlike the sterile. Spore cases bead-like and arranged in two rows as shown in Figures 1 and 3. Fruits in late summer.

Stipe porous and free from scales. Figure 2 shows a cross section of the stipe. Vascular bundles unite at top of stipe.

Habitat—Wet places, either in woods or open meadows. Common.

Remarks—It can be distinguished from the Net-veined Chain-fern, with which it is often confused, by its almost triangular blade. No doubt it is called "sensitive" because it is quite easily killed by the frost.

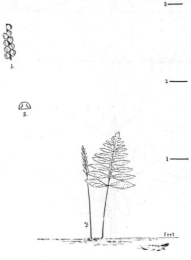

19

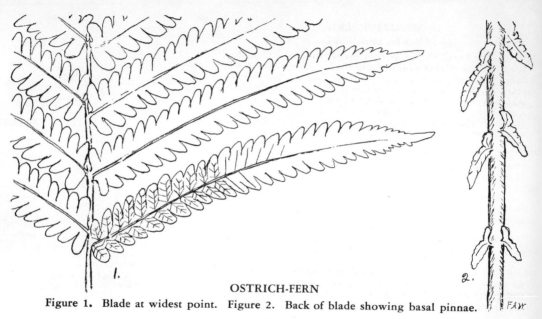

OSTRICH-FERN

Figure 1. Blade at widest point. Figure 2. Back of blade showing basal pinnae.

20

OSTRICH-FERN

(Pteretis nodulosa (Michx.) Nieuwl.), or
(Onoclea Struthiopteris (L.) Hoffm.), or
(Matteuccia Struthiopteris (L.) Todaro)

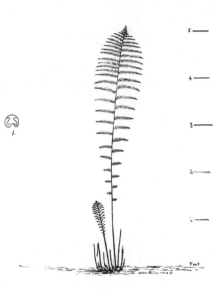

Sterile frond shown was 34½ inches long, and 9 inches broad above the center of the blade. Sometimes 7 or 8 feet long. Fronds abruptly narrowed at the top; coarse in texture; erect; clustered. Figure 1 on page 20 shows the long narrow pinnae at the widest point of the blade, while Figure 2 shows the back of the very short pinnae at the base. Note how the first lobe turns back over the rachis.

Fertile frond was 12 inches long; stiffly erect; brownish and formed like an ostrich plume. Fruits in late summer.

Figure 1 shows a cross section of the stipe. Stipe deeply grooved; scaleless; dark brown at the base. Vascular bundles usually outlined by dark brown.

Habitat—Rich wet woods and forest. More common in northern part of range.

Remarks—The very small basal pinnae will serve to distinguish it from either the Cinnamon or Interrupted ferns with which it is often confused.

21

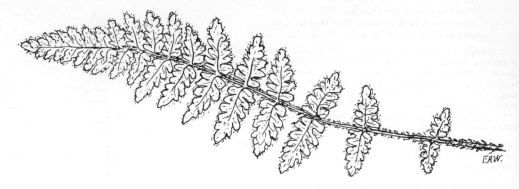

RUSTY WOODSIA
(Woodsia ilvensis (L.) R. Br.)

Three to eleven inches long bearing spore sacs in small clusters (sori) on the back of the blade. The under surface is so covered by rusty chaff that it is difficult to see the sori. Stipe jointed near base. Upper surface showing scattered hairs. Usually found at an altitude of 1000 feet or higher. More common northward. Grows in dense tufts, on ledges which may be quite dry at times causing the fronds to roll up, particularly in late summer.

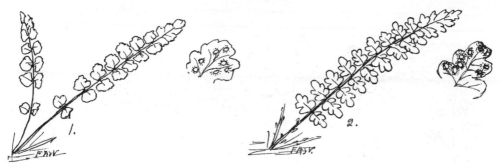

FIGURE 1.   SMOOTH WOODSIA
(Woodsia glabella R. Br.)

Very small and delicate. Smooth and green throughout. Lower pinnae usually widely spaced. Stipe jointed near base. Moist ledges.

FIGURE 2.   ALPINE WOODSIA
(Woodsia alpina (Bolton) S. F. Gray)

Small and delicate. Sightly chaffy beneath. Stipe jointed and light brown at base. Both forms rare. Found at high altitudes on moist ledges. Both grow in tufts. Range for both, northern New York northward.

23

1.   2.

BLUNT-LOBED WOODSIA
(Woodsia obtusa (Spreng.) Torr.)

Fronds 15—20 inches long. Veins covered with scattered hairs throughout. Pinnae blunt. Figure 1 shows the position of the sori on the under surface of the blade. Figure 2 shows a cross section of the stipe. The vascular bundles are light in color. Grows in tufts on ledges or on rocky hillsides. The jointed scaly stipe and scaly rachis serve to distinguish it from the Brittle-fern.

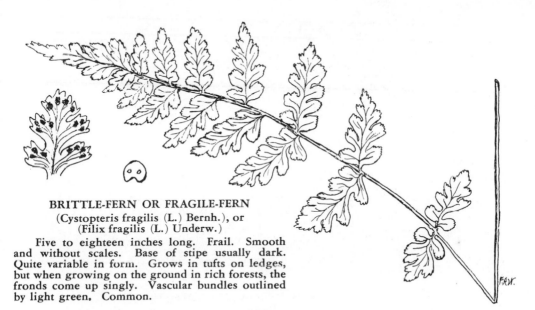

BRITTLE-FERN OR FRAGILE-FERN

(Cystopteris fragilis (L.) Bernh.), or
(Filix fragilis (L.) Underw.)

Five to eighteen inches long. Frail. Smooth
and without scales. Base of stipe usually dark.
Quite variable in form. Grows in tufts on ledges,
but when growing on the ground in rich forests, the
fronds come up singly. Vascular bundles outlined
by light green. Common.

25

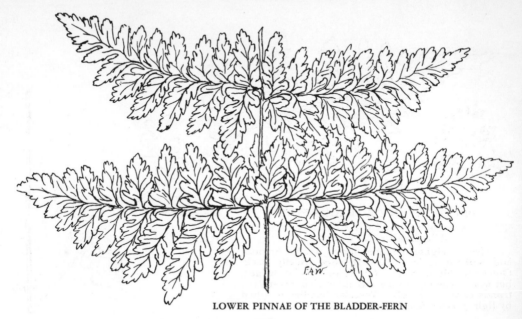

LOWER PINNAE OF THE BLADDER-FERN

26

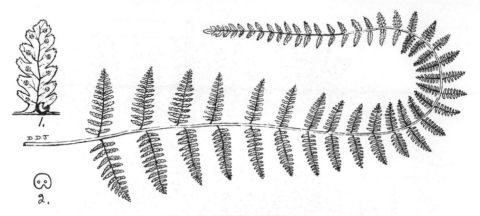

BLADDER-FERN

(Cystopteris bulbifera (L.) Bernh.), or (Filix bulbifera (L.) Underw.)

This fertile frond was reduced from a 27 inch specimen, while the lower pinnae of the 8 inch sterile frond are shown in full size, on page 26. Fronds delicate, drooping. This fern reproduces by means of spores, and also by bulblets which drop and grow into new plants. The bulblets form at the axis of the veins of pinnae and pinnules, see Figure 1. Figure 2 shows a cross section of the stipe. The vascular bundles are light in color. Grows on wet ledges. The extremely long tapering fruiting fronds are a good field mark.

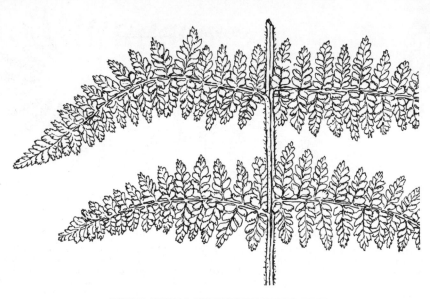

LOWER PINNAE OF THE HAYSCENTED FERN

HAYSCENTED OR BOULDER-FERN

(Dennstaedtia punctilobula (Michx.) Moore), or
(Dicksonia punctilobula (Michx.) Gray)

Frond shown was 24½ inches long, and 7½ inches
broad the third pinna from base. Sometimes twice this
size. Fronds thin in texture; erect; single or loosely
clustered. Page 28 shows the lower pinnae.

Stipe and rachis covered with short hairs. Stipe
often dark brown at base. Figure 2 shows a cross
section of the stipe. The vascular bundles are light in
color.

Figure 1 shows the small, cup-shaped spore cases
which grow at the axis of the notches. Fruits in summer.

Habitat—Open fields, thin woods, hillsides, in
quite varied habitats. Common.

Remarks—The sword-shaped blade, very finely cut
margins, the hairy stipe and rachis, and the fact that the
blades turn to face the light, are good field marks. It is
fragrant when crushed.

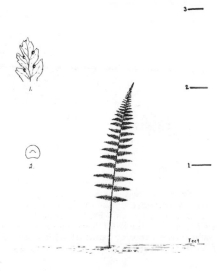

29

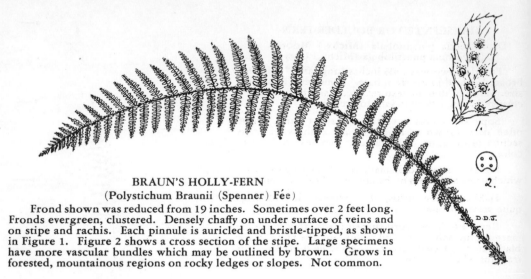

BRAUN'S HOLLY-FERN
(Polystichum Braunii (Spenner) Fée)

Frond shown was reduced from 19 inches. Sometimes over 2 feet long. Fronds evergreen, clustered. Densely chaffy on under surface of veins and on stipe and rachis. Each pinnule is auricled and bristle-tipped, as shown in Figure 1. Figure 2 shows a cross section of the stipe. Large specimens have more vascular bundles which may be outlined by brown. Grows in forested, mountainous regions on rocky ledges or slopes. Not common.

CHRISTMAS FERN
(Polystichum acrostichoides (Michx.) Schott)

Fertile frond 15 inches to 2½ feet long. Sterile frond usually much shorter than the fertile. Both fronds may be somewhat longer than this. Evergreen, clustered. Pinna auricled and stalked. Edges of pinna usually toothed, but variable.

Spore cases are borne in dense clusters on the abruptly shortened pinnae at the top of the blade, as shown in Figure 1. Fruits in summer.

Stipe and rachis covered with light brown scales, which are larger and more plentiful at the base. Figure 2 shows a cross section of the stipe. The vascular bundles are transluscent, outlined by light green.

Habitat—Rocky hillsides in woods. Common.

Remarks—The pinnae are the shape of "Christmas stockings."

31

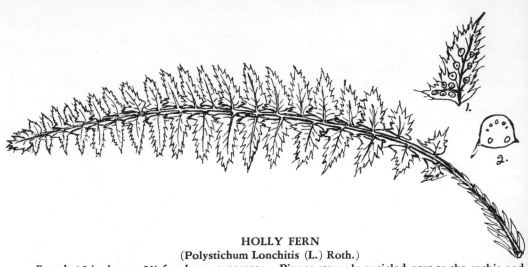

HOLLY FERN
(Polystichum Lonchitis (L.) Roth.)

Fronds 15 inches to 2½ feet long, evergreen. Pinnae strongly auricled next to the rachis and spiny margined. Lower pinnae mostly triangular. Stipe, rachis and veins scaly. The scales of the stipe large, cinnamon colored and dense. This fern grows in rocky forested areas in Gaspé, near Niagara Falls, northern Michigan and other northern regions. It is included here for comparative purposes.

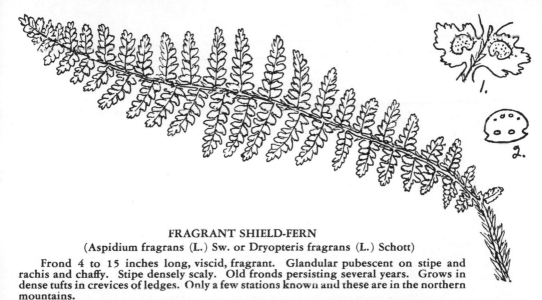

FRAGRANT SHIELD-FERN
(Aspidium fragrans (L.) Sw. or Dryopteris fragrans (L.) Schott)

Frond 4 to 15 inches long, viscid, fragrant. Glandular pubescent on stipe and rachis and chaffy. Stipe densely scaly. Old fronds persisting several years. Grows in dense tufts in crevices of ledges. Only a few stations known and these are in the northern mountains.

Remarks—The fronds are so viscid they adhere to each other when gathered.

33

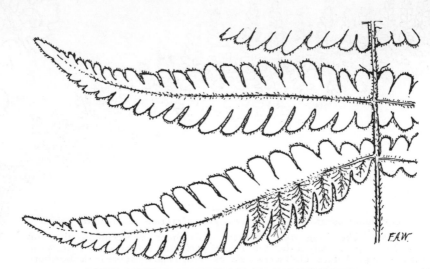

LOWER PORTION OF THE BLADE OF LONG BEECH-FERN

34

LONG BEECH-FERN

(Phegopteris Phegopteris (L.) Keyserl.), or
(Phegopteris polypodioides Fée), or
(Dryopteris Phegopteris (L.) C. Chr.)

Frond shown was 19 inches long and 7½ inches broad. Fronds thin in texture, single. Blade set at an angle to the rachis; hairy above and below on the veins. Page 34 shows lower pinnae. On smaller specimens the rachis may be winged between second and third pinnae and on to the top.

Sori small, near the margin of the forked veins, without indusia. Usually quite numerous, as shown in Figure 1. Fruits in summer.

Stipe and rachis covered by fine, hair-like scales. Figure 2 shows a cross section of the stipe. Vascular bundles outlined in brown and united at top of stipe.

Habitat—On ground in rich forests.

Remarks—Can be distinguished from Broad Beech-fern, with which it is often confused, by the narrower lower pinnae, hairy veins, and more elongated blade. The two lower pinnae usually stand up in front of the rest of the blade.

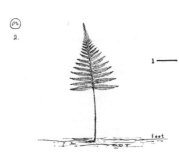

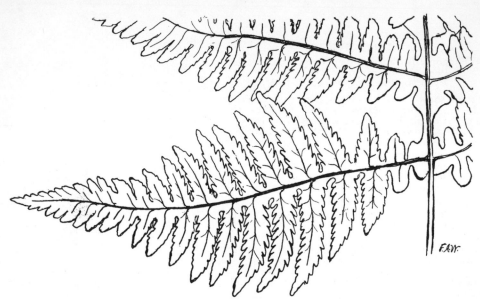

LOWER PINNA OF THE BROAD BEECH-FERN

BROAD BEECH-FERN

(Phegopteris hexagonoptera (Michx.) Fée), or
(Dryopteris hexagonoptera (Michx.) C. Chr.)

Frond shown was 15 inches long, and 9 inches broad. Sometimes longer. Fronds single. Blade thin in texture; stands at an angle to the stipe; often somewhat glandular beneath. Page 36 shows lower pinna and winged rachis.

Sori near the margin as shown in Figure 1. Fruits in summer.

Stipe and rachis free from scales except at base. Figure 2 shows a cross section of the stipe. Vascular bundles light green and united at top of stipe.

Habitat—Grows on the ground in rich, moist woods and forests.

Remarks—Note that the lower pinna is quite broad in the center. Lower pinnae often stand up in front of the rest of the blade.

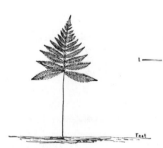

37

OAK-FERN

(Phegopteris Dryopteris (L.) Fée), or (Dryopteris Dryopteris (L.) Britton)

Frond shown was 10¾ inches long and 6 inches broad. Sometimes 18 inches long. Fronds single; blade set at right angle to the stipe; thin in texture. Frail. Stipe and rachis free from scales. Stipe dark at base. Vascular bundles outlined in dark brown. Grows on ground, in forests of mountainous regions. More common northward.

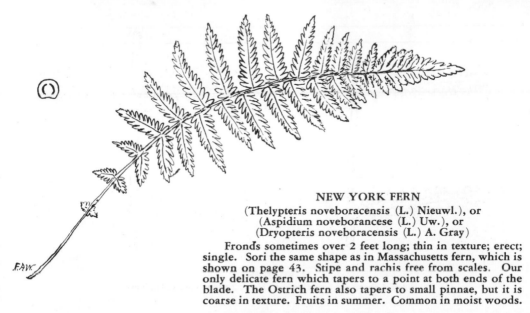

NEW YORK FERN

(Thelypteris noveboracensis (L.) Nieuwl.), or
(Aspidium noveborancese (L.) Uw.), or
(Dryopteris noveboracensis (L.) A. Gray)

Fronds sometimes over 2 feet long; thin in texture; erect; single. Sori the same shape as in Massachusetts fern, which is shown on page 43. Stipe and rachis free from scales. Our only delicate fern which tapers to a point at both ends of the blade. The Ostrich fern also tapers to small pinnae, but it is coarse in texture. Fruits in summer. Common in moist woods.

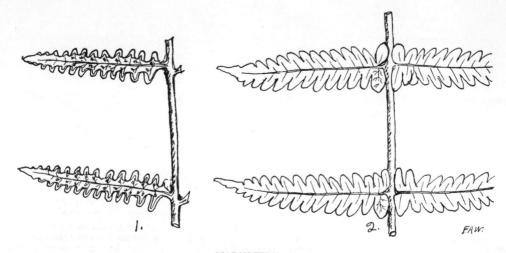

MARSH-FERN
Figure 1 shows the fertile pinnae. Figure 2 shows the sterile pinnae.

MARSH-FERN

(Thelypteris Thelypteris (L.) Nieuwl.), or
(Aspidium Thelypteris (L.) Sw.), or
(Dryopteris Thelypteris (L.) A. Gray)

Fertile frond shown was 21½ inches long, and 4 inches broad at the widest point; longer than the sterile. The segments are rolled under, covering many of the spore cases. Fruits in late summer.

Sterile frond was 19½ inches long, and 4⅜ inches broad at the widest point. The veinlets in the segments are forked. Figure 1 shows the fertile, and Figure 2 shows the sterile segments.

Stipe and rachis free from scales. Figure 3 shows a cross section of the stipe. Vascular bundles outlined in dark brown, united at top of stipe.

Habitat—Marshes, and hillsides if sufficiently wet.

Remarks—The pinnae are usually widely spaced, and the veinlets forked. The forked veinlets throughout the entire sterile blade will serve to separate this species from the Massachusetts fern with which it is often confused.

41

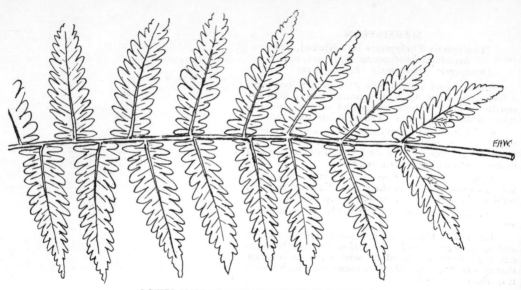

LOWER HALF OF MASSACHUSETTS OR BOG-FERN

MASSACHUSETTS OR BOG-FERN

(Thelypteris simulata (Davenp.) Nieuwl.), or
(Aspidium simulatum Davenp.), or
(Dryopteris simulata Davenp.)

Frond shown was 24 inches long and 3 inches broad. Sometimes smaller. Frond thin in texture, single. Page 42 shows the lower part of a rather typical frond. There is much variation in shape. The lower pinnae usually stand up in front of the rest of the blade. Segments are entire and the veinlets are never branched in the upper portion of the sterile blade. They may sometimes be branched in the lower portion of the blade. Figure 1 shows the straight venation and the placement of the sori. Fruits in summer.

Stipe and rachis have scattered scales which are shed early. Figure 2 shows a cross section of the stipe. No dark outline to vascular bundles, unite near base of stipe.

Habitat—Marshy areas. Not common.

Remarks—Often confused with New York and Marsh-fern. The New York fern tapers to a point at both ends of the blade while the Marsh-fern and Massachusetts do not. The Marsh-fern has forked veinlets while the Massachusetts fern never has forked veinlets at the top of the blade. The bluish-green fronds of the Marsh-fern are distinct from the bright green of the Bog-fern. Found as far north as Maine.

43

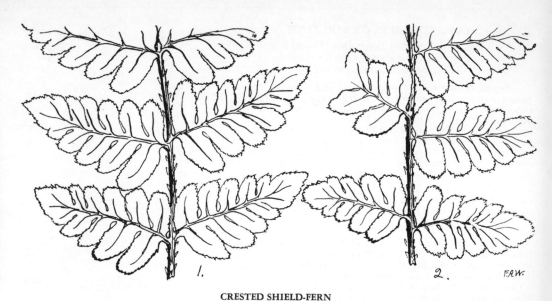

CRESTED SHIELD-FERN
Figure 1. Lower pinnae of sterile blade.   Figure 2. Lower pinnae of fertile blade.

44

CRESTED SHIELD-FERN

(Dryopteris cristata (L.) A. Gray), or
(Aspidium cristatum (L.) Sw.)

Fertile frond was 21 inches long and 2½ inches broad. Fronds thick in texture; erect; clustered. Figure 2 on page 44 shows the fertile pinnae. They are smaller than the sterile pinnae and the fronds are much taller. The pinnae are bluish-green.

Sterile frond shown was 11 inches long and 3¼ inches broad. Both sterile and fertile fronds are sometimes several inches taller than given. The sterile pinnae are shown in Figure 1 on page 44.

Sori large and covered by a kidney-shaped indusium. Fruits in summer.

Stipe and rachis covered with brown scales which are larger and more plentiful at the base of the stipe. Stipe grooved. Figure 2 shows a cross section of the stipe. Vascular bundles outlined in brown.

Habitat—Marshes. Common.

Remarks—Often confused with Clinton's fern which is usually wider, taller, and the lower pinnae longer in proportion to the width. More common than Clinton's.

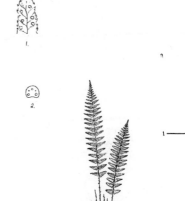

45

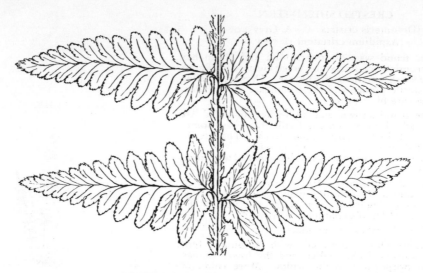

LOWER PINNAE OF CLINTON'S FERN

CLINTON'S FERN

(Dryopteris Clintoniana D. C. Eaton) Dowell), or
(Aspidium cristatum var. Clintonianum D. C. Eaton)

Frond shown was 19 inches long, and 6 inches broad about the center of the blade. Sometimes 4 feet or more long. Fronds evergreen; clustered. Fertile blade not much longer than the sterile. Figure 2 on page 46 shows the lower pinnae.

Sori nearer the midvein than the margin, as shown in Figure 1. Indusium kidney-shaped and without glands. Fruits in summer.

Stipe and rachis covered by light brown scales which are larger and more plentiful at the base of the stipe. Stipe grooved. Figure 2 shows cross section of stipe.

Habitat—Marshes of forested areas. Not common.

Remarks—Sometimes confused with Goldie's fern, but the triangular basal pinna is quite easily distinguished from the long, lower pinna of Goldie's which is broadest in the center. The sori are nearer the midvein than are those of the crested Shield-fern. See remarks about the Crested Shield-fern on page 45. The texture of Clinton's fern is not as heavy as the Crested Shield. It being a distinct species is questionable.

47

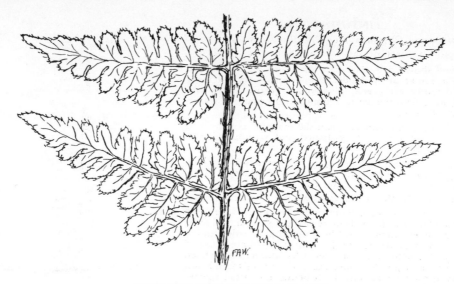

THE LOWER PINNAE OF BOOTT'S FERN

BOOT'S FERN

(Dryopteris Boottii (Tuckm.) Underw.), or
(Aspidium Boottii Tuckm.)

Frond shown was 26 inches long and 5 inches wide. Sometimes 4 feet or more long. Fronds evergreen; clustered. Sterile frond usually shorter. Page 48 shows lower pinnae. Figure 1 shows the placement of the sori. The indusium is sparingly glandular. Fruits in summer.

Stipe and rachis covered with light brown scales which are more plentiful at the base of the stipe. Figure 2 shows the vascular bundles. They are outlined by dark brown. Stipe grooved.

Habitat—Wet forests or marshes.

Remarks—Texture is a little less thick than that of crested shield-fern and the margins are more spiny and more deeply incised, as in Spineulose Shield-fern. It being a distinct species is questionable.

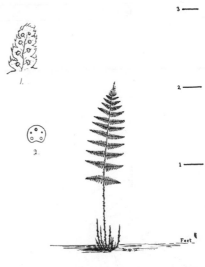

49

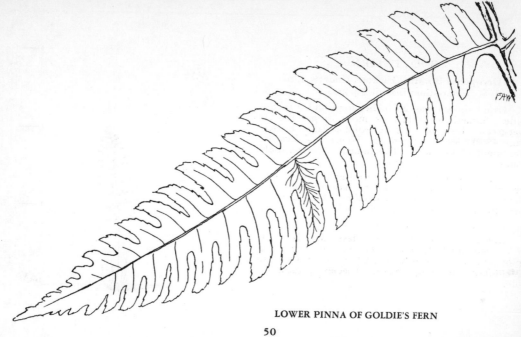

LOWER PINNA OF GOLDIE'S FERN

50

GOLDIE'S FERN

(Dryopteris Goldiana (Hook.) A. Gray), or
(Aspidium Goldianum Hook.)

Frond shown was 22 inches long and 10¾ inches broad. Sterile and fertile fronds about the same size. Sometimes more than twice this size. Fronds not evergreen; single or loosely clustered. Pinna broadest in the center. Segments usually somewhat hooked and sparingly toothed.

Sori are situated in regular series very near the midvein, as shown in Figure 1. Fruits in summer.

Stipe and rachis covered by large, dark brown scales at the base, shading to lighter brown above. Figure 2 shows a cross section of the stipe. Note that there are 7 vascular bundles. Stipe grooved.

Habitat—Ravines or rocky hillsides in rich forests. More common in mountainous regions.

Remarks—The very broad outline of the blade, coupled with the shape of the lower pinna will serve to distinguish this species.

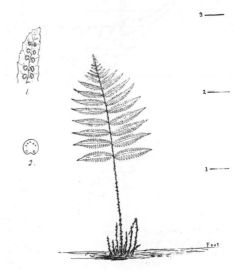

51

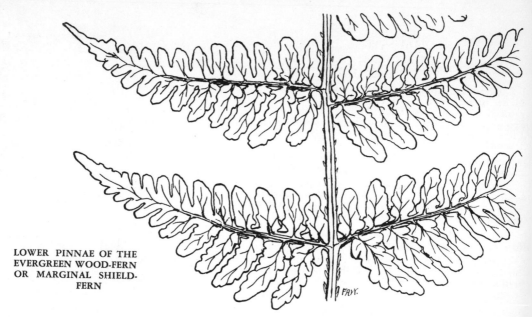

LOWER PINNAE OF THE
EVERGREEN WOOD-FERN
OR MARGINAL SHIELD-
FERN

FRYY.

EVERGREEN WOOD-FERN OR MARGINAL SHIELD-FERN

(Dryopteris marginalis (L.) A. Gray), or
(Aspidium marginale (L.) Sw.)

Frond shown was 22 inches long and 8½ inches broad. Widest, fifth pinnae from the base. Sometimes 3 feet long. Fronds almost leathery in texture; clustered. The lower pinnae are shown on page 52. Veins blue-green. Segments without teeth. Figure 1 shows a segment and the large sori almost on the margin. Fruits in summer.

Stipe and rachis densely covered with long, chestnut-brown scales which grow smaller in size and more scattered above. Figure 2 shows a cross section of the stipe. The 7 vascular bundles are outlined in brown. Stipe grooved.

Habitat—Rocky slopes; usually in thickly forested areas.

Remarks—The large marginal sori; the very long, dense, basal scales; the thick texture; and the spineless segments will serve to identify this fern.

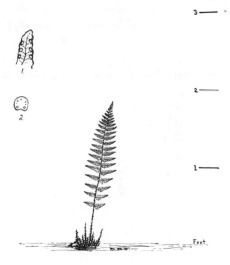

53

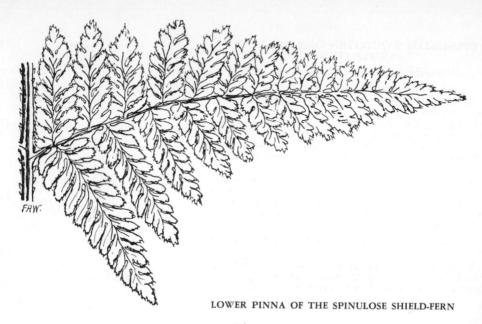

LOWER PINNA OF THE SPINULOSE SHIELD-FERN

SPINULOSE SHIELD-FERN OR TOOTHED WOOD-FERN

(Dryopteris spinulosa (Muell.) Kuntze), or

(Aspidium spinulosum (O. F. Muell.) Sw.)

Frond shown was 26 inches long and 9½ inches broad. Sometimes 3 feet long. Fronds not evergreen; clustered. The lower pinna is shown on page 54. The longest pinna is about the center of the blade. Note the elongated pinnule next to the stipe. Pinnules with sharp teeth. Teeth turn inward.

Sori small, kidney-shaped indusium without glands. Figure 1 shows a portion of a pinnule and the placement of the sori. Fruits in summer.

Stipe and rachis covered with scattered scales which are light brown and often dark-centered. Scales more plentiful at base of stipe. Stipe grooved. Vascular bundles light, outlined by brown.

Habitat—Rich, moist or wet woods and forests. More common northward.

Remarks—Sometimes confused with the Spreading Shield-fern which also has the first pinnule, next to the rachis, elongated. The Spinulose Shield-fern is more narrow in proportion to the width of the blade, and the pinnae have a decided tendency to turn upward.

55

LOWER PINNA OF THE SPREADING SHIELD-FERN

SPREADING SHIELD-FERN

(Dryopteris campyloptera (Kunze) Clarkson), or
(Aspidium spinulosum var. dilatatum (Hoffm.)
Hook.), or (Dryopteris dilatata (Hoffm.) Gray)

Frond shown was 25 inches long and 9½ inches broad. This is rather a small frond. They are sometimes 3½ feet long or more. Fronds not evergreen; clustered. The lower pinna is shown on page 56. Note the much elongated pinnule next to the rachis. Pinnules sharp toothed as shown in Figure 1.

Sori are kidney-shaped; small and without glands. Fruits in summer.

Stipe and rachis covered with light brown scales which are more plentiful at the base of the stipe. Figure 2 shows a cross section of the stipe. The vascular bundles are outlined in brown. A 34 inch specimen had seven bundles. Stipe grooved.

Habitat—Rich, moist woods, more common in the mountainous regions.

Remarks—The blade is very broad in comparison to its length, and the first pinnule is much elongated. The blade of the drawing at the right should be shorter in proportion to the width.

57

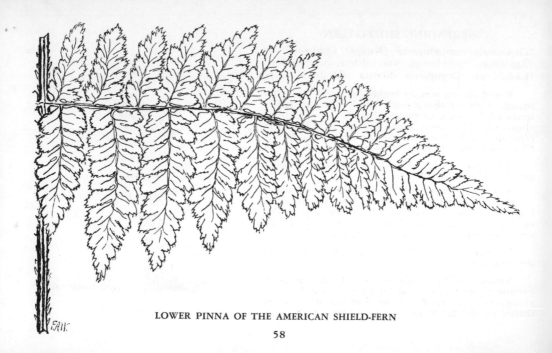

LOWER PINNA OF THE AMERICAN SHIELD-FERN

AMERICAN SHIELD-FERN

(Dryopteris intermedia (Muhl.) A. Gray), or
(Aspidium spinulosum var. intermedium (Muhl.)
D. C. Eaton)

Frond shown was 27 inches long, and 10 inches broad near the base of the blade. Sometimes 2½ feet long. Fronds evergreen; clustered. Lower pinna shown on page 58. Note the elongated second pinnule.

Sori small. Glandular indusia as shown in Figure 2. Figure 1 shows a section of a pinnule and the placement of the sori. Fruits in summer.

Stipe and rachis thinly covered with dark-centered, light brown scales which are more plentiful at the base. Figure 3 shows a cross section of the stipe. The vascular bundles are outlined in brown and quite irregular in number.

Habitat—Moist or wet woods and forests. Common except on higher mountains.

Remarks—Can be distinguished almost always by the elongated second pinnule. This is the fern which is so commonly used with cut flowers by florists.

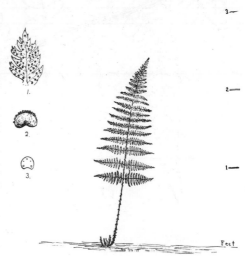

59

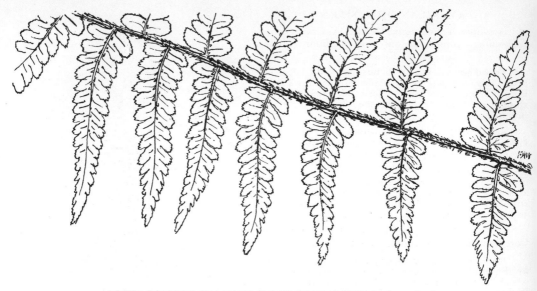

LOWER PORTION OF A SMALL FROND OF MALE FERN (under surface)

MALE FERN

(Dryopteris Filix-mas (L.) Schott), or
(Aspidium Filix-mas (L.) Sw.)

Frond shown was 30 inches long, and 7 inches broad above the center of the blade. Sometimes 3½ to 4 feet long. Fronds erect; clustered. Page 60 shows the lower portion of a small frond. Note the narrow, elongated, sword-shaped pinnae. Pinnules and segments finely cut at the tips.
Sori kidney-shaped, and nearer the midvein than the margin. Indusium without glands. Fruits in summer.

Stipe and rachis thickly covered with light brown scales. Central vein of the pinna also scaly. Figure 2 shows a cross section of the stipe. Vascular bundles outlined in brown. Stipe grooved.

Habitat—Rocky, moist forests. Found only in the extreme northern part of the range.

Remarks—The sword-shaped pinnae, coupled with the very scaly stipe and rachis, will serve as good field marks.

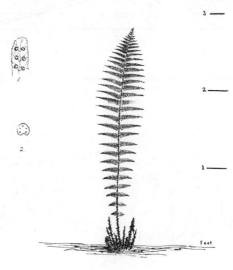

61

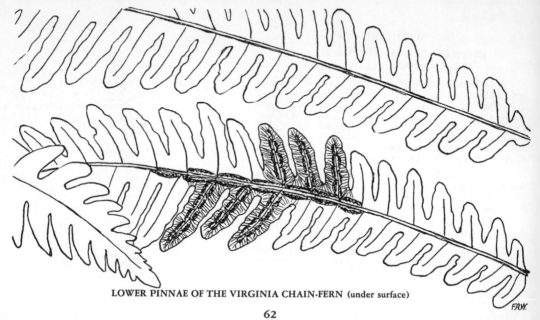

LOWER PINNAE OF THE VIRGINIA CHAIN-FERN (under surface)

VIRGINIA CHAIN-FERN

(Anchistea virginica (L.) Presl), or
(Woodwardia virginica (L.) Sm.)

Frond shown was 29 inches long, and 7 inches broad at the base of the blade. Sometimes 6 feet long. Fronds coarse in texture; erect; single. Page 62 shows the under surface of the lower pinnae. Note the spore cases in long chain-like formation. Fruits in late summer.

Stipe and rachis free from scales. Dark brown at base. Figure 1 shows a cross section of the stipe and the 7 vascular bundles. Large fronds have 9 bundles, outlined by dark brown.

Habitat—Marshes, many times in the water. Not common.

Remarks—Sterile fronds might be confused with Cinnamon or Interrupted ferns. Look for the chain-like venation of the Chain-fern.

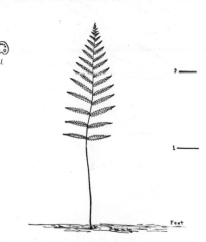

63

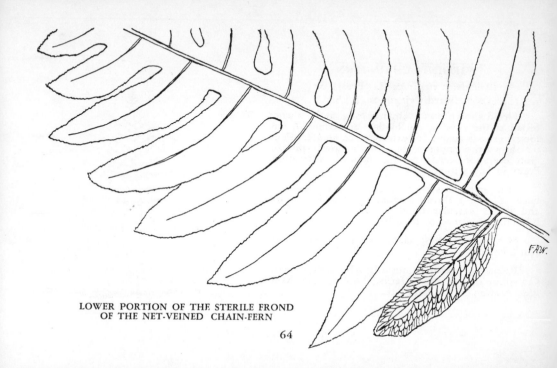

LOWER PORTION OF THE STERILE FROND
OF THE NET-VEINED CHAIN-FERN

64

NET-VEINED CHAIN-FERN

(Lorinseria areolata (L.) Presl), or
(Woodwardia areolata (L.) Moore)

Sterile frond shown on page 64 was 12 inches long. They are sometimes 3 feet long. Sterile fronds thin in texture; erect; single.

Fertile frond very unlike the sterile. Stiff; erect; segments narrow, bearing chain-like spore cases, as shown in Figures 2 and 3. Fruits in midsummer.

Stipe shining and brownish at the base, winged at top. Figure 1 shows cross section of stipe. The vascular bundles are outlined in brown and unite at the top of stipe.

Habitat—Swamps. More common in southern half of range.

Remarks—Often confused with Sensitive fern. The Sensitive is always more triangular in outline and the lobes are opposite.

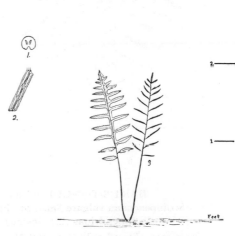

65

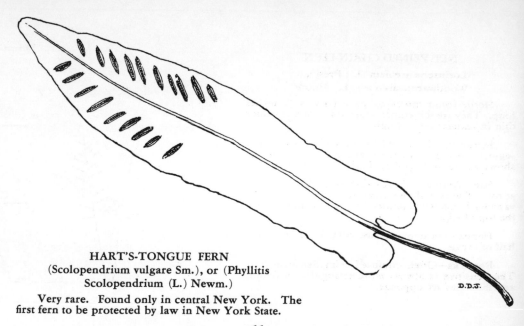

HART'S-TONGUE FERN
(Scolopendrium vulgare Sm.), or (Phyllitis
Scolopendrium (L.) Newm.)

Very rare. Found only in central New York. The
first fern to be protected by law in New York State.

D.D.J.

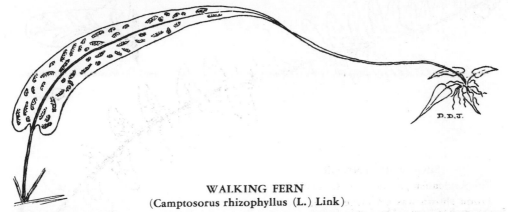

WALKING FERN
(Camptosorus rhizophyllus (L.) Link)

The entire-edged frond with its long tapering tip is enough to identify this species. It reproduces by means of spores, and also by the ends of the fronds taking root. Hence the name "walking fern." The spore cases are irregularly placed on the under surface. The vascular bundles are outlined in brown.

Habitat—Trails over ledges—usually limestone.

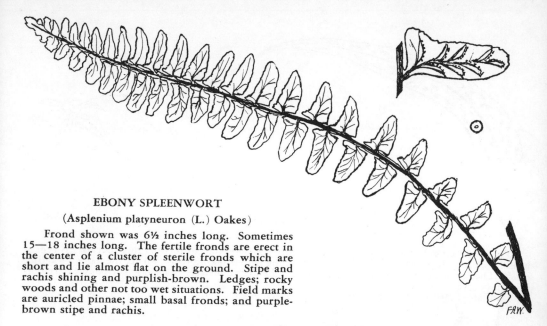

EBONY SPLEENWORT

(Asplenium platyneuron (L.) Oakes)

Frond shown was 6½ inches long. Sometimes 15—18 inches long. The fertile fronds are erect in the center of a cluster of sterile fronds which are short and lie almost flat on the ground. Stipe and rachis shining and purplish-brown. Ledges; rocky woods and other not too wet situations. Field marks are auricled pinnae; small basal fronds; and purple-brown stipe and rachis.

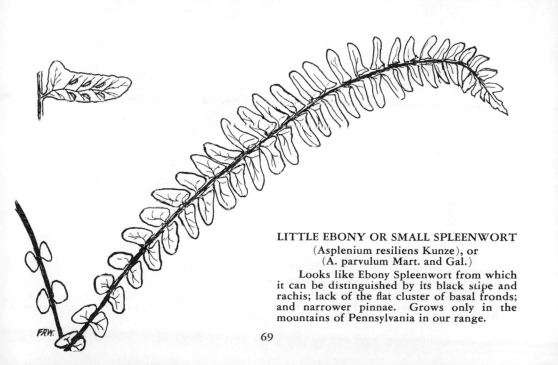

LITTLE EBONY OR SMALL SPLEENWORT
(Asplenium resiliens Kunze), or
(A. parvulum Mart. and Gal.)

Looks like Ebony Spleenwort from which it can be distinguished by its black stipe and rachis; lack of the flat cluster of basal fronds; and narrower pinnae. Grows only in the mountains of Pennsylvania in our range.

FRW.

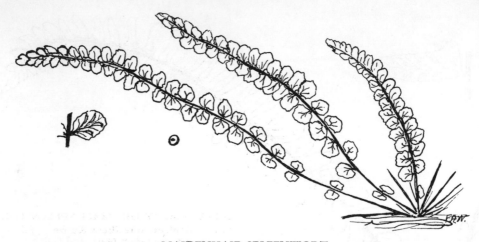

MAIDENHAIR SPLEENWORT
(Asplenium Trichomanes L.)

Fronds up to 10 inches long. Pinnae almost round and toothed at the top. Stipe and rachis purplish-brown, blackish scales below. Grows on ledges in dense tufts. Commonly found in cracks under overhanging ledges where there is plenty of moisture.

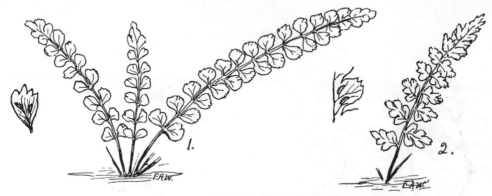

Figure 1. GREEN SPLEENWORT
(Asplenium viride Huds.)

Might be confused with Maidenhair Spleenwort from which it can be distinguished by the green rachis and upper portion of the stipe. Found only in mountains northward. Rare.

Figure 2. BRADLEY'S SPLEENWORT
(Asplenium Bradleyi D. C. Eaton)

Pinnae are wedge-shaped. Stipe dark brown. Very local and rare. Mountains in southern part of range.

WALL-RUE
(Asplenium cryptolepis Fernald), or
(A. Ruta-muraria L.)

Fronds 2—9 inches long. Green throughout. Grows in dense tufts on limestone. The wedge-shaped, stalked divisions, which are toothed, are good field marks. Not common.

Found in center and southern part of range.

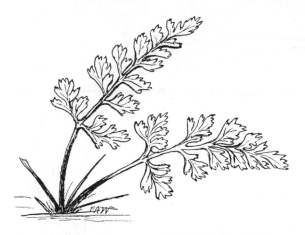

MOUNTAIN SPLEENWORT
(Asplenium montanum Willd.)

Fronds 2—6 inches long. Stipe dark brown about ⅔ of the way to the blade. 2—3 teeth to each division. Grows in tufts on mossy ledges in mountainous regions. Found only in central and southern portion of range. Confused with Wall-rue from which it can be distinguished by its dark stipe and more deeply toothed margin.

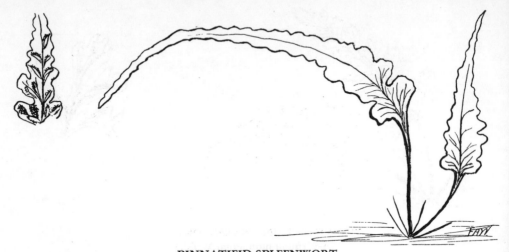

PINNATIFID SPLEENWORT
(Asplenium pinnatifidum Nutt.)

Fronds 3—15 inches long, rather thick in texture. Variously lobed but never cut to the midvein. Stipe dark brown. Grows in tufts on ledges. Rare and found only in the southern portion of range.

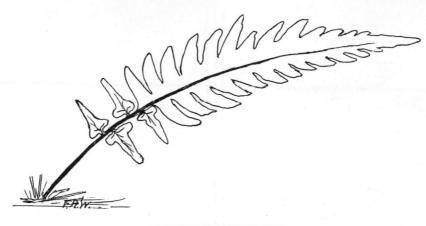

SCOTT'S SPLEENWORT
(Asplenium ebenoides R. R. Scott)

Fronds 3—15 inches long. Blade nearly always cut, at least once, to the midvein and sometimes oftener. Stipe and about ⅔ of the rachis dark brown. Very rare, only a few stations known in range. Probably a hybrid between Walking-fern and Ebony Spleenwort.

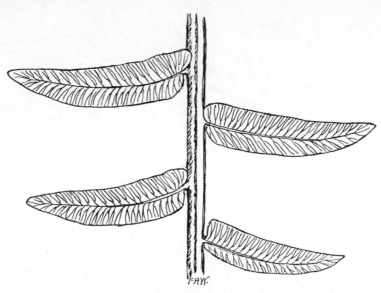

LOWER PINNAE OF GLADE-FERN OR NARROW-LEAVED SPLEENWORT

GLADE-FERN OR NARROW-LEAVED SPLEENWORT

(Homalosorus pycnocarpus (Spreng.) Small), or
(Asplenium angustifolium Michx.), or
(A. pycnocarpon Spreng.)

Frond shown was 21 inches long and 5½ inches broad. Sometimes 3 feet or more long. Fronds thin in texture; erect; clustered. The width of fertile blade narrower than the sterile. Page 76 shows the lower pinnae.

Sori slightly curved, attached at one side and very regularly placed, as shown in Figure 1. Fruits in summer.

Stipe dark at base and free from scales. Figure 2 shows a cross section of the stipe. The vascular bundles may unite at top of stipe.

Habitat—Ravines or rocky hillsides in rich forests. More common in mountainous sections.

Remarks—Often found growing in company with Goldie's-fern. Might be confused with Christmas fern, but is thinner in texture. Also the pinnae of the Christmas have toothed margins and are auricled.

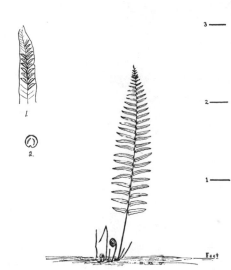

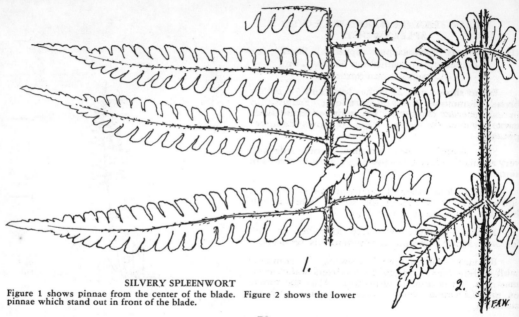

SILVERY SPLEENWORT

Figure 1 shows pinnae from the center of the blade. Figure 2 shows the lower pinnae which stand out in front of the blade.

SILVERY SPLEENWORT

(Diplazium acrostichoides (Sw.) Butters), or
(Asplenium acrostichoides Sw.), or
(Athyrium thelypteroides (Michx.) Desv.)

Frond shown was 41½ inches long, and 11½ inches broad about the center of the blade. Often 4 feet long. Fronds somewhat thin in texture; erect; clustered. Central pinnae shown in Figure 1, on page 78 and lower pinnae, which stand out in front of the blade, are shown in Figure 2. Segments appear almost square-cut at the end.

Sori silvery and prominent as shown in Figure 1. Fruits in early summer.

Stipe, rachis and veins quite hairy. Figure 2 shows a cross section of the stipe, which has light colored vascular bundles that may, or may not, unite at top of stipe.

Habitat—Swampy areas in rich woods. Not common in northern part of range.

Remarks—Sometimes confused with Lady-fern from which it can be distinguished by its hairy stipe and rachis, and less cut pinnae.

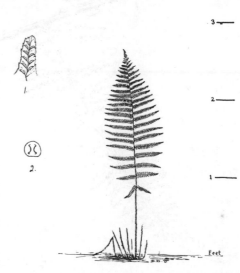

79

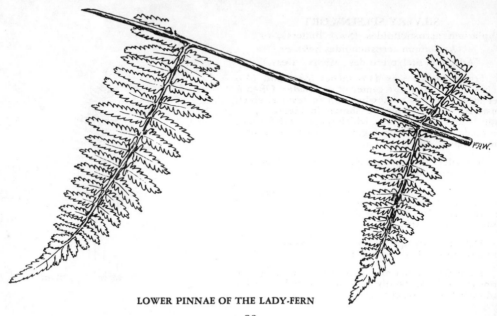

LOWER PINNAE OF THE LADY-FERN

LADY-FERN
(Athyrium asplenioides (Michx.) Desv.), or
(Asplenium Filix-femina (L.) Bernh.), or
(Athyrium Filix-foemina (L.) Roth)

Frond shown was 20 inches long, and 8 inches broad at the center of the blade. Sometimes twice this size. Fronds rather thin in texture; erect; clustered. Lower pinnae are shown on page 80. The lower pair usually stand up in front of the blade.

Sori, especially near base of pinnae, curved as shown in Figure 1. Fruits in early summer.

Stipe covered at base with black-centered scales which drop off early. Figure 2 shows a cross section of the stipe which has light colored vascular bundles which may be outlined in black and occasionally unite at top of stipe.

Habitat—Quite variable but grows to best advantage in moist woods or forests.

Remarks—The lower pinnae projecting forward; the blade broadest at about the center; and the scaleless rachis will serve to distinguish it from the Hayscented Fern, with which it is often confused. Very variable in form. Dr. J. K. Small and others recognize two species, the Upland and the Lowland Lady-fern.

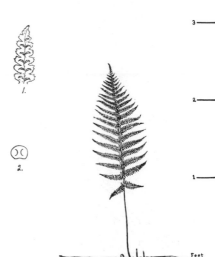

81

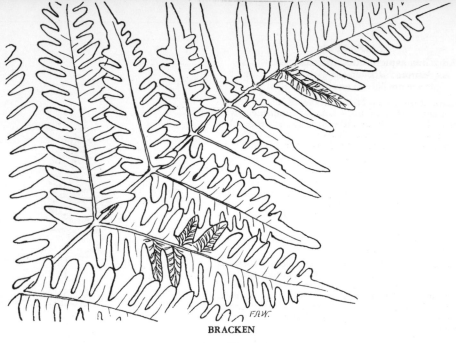

BRACKEN

BRACKEN OR BRAKE-FERN

(Pteris latiuscula Desv.), or (P. aquilina L.), or (Pteridium aquilinum (L.) Kuhn.)

Frond shown was almost 4 feet long when laid out flat. Sometimes much longer. Fronds very coarse in texture; erect; single. The three-parted triangular blade stands at right angles to the stipe. Page 82 shows the upper section of one of the triangles.

Fertile frond has the edges of the segments turned under. The rolled edges hide the spore cases. Fruits in late summer.

Stipe and rachis free from scales. Figure 2 shows a cross section of the stipe. Note the many vascular bundles, their irregularity and number.

Habitat—Open woods and fields. Almost everywhere. Common.

Remarks—Its thick, coarse texture will serve to distinguish it from other triangular forms, even when the Bracken is young. Found almost throughout the world.

83

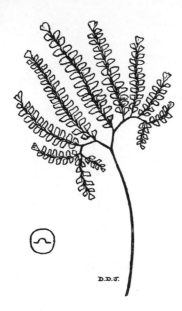

MAIDENHAIR-FERN
(Adiantum pedatum L.)

Fronds up to 1 or 3 feet long. Thin in texture. The only fern we have which is palmately branched. Stipe and rachis purplish-brown, and shiny.

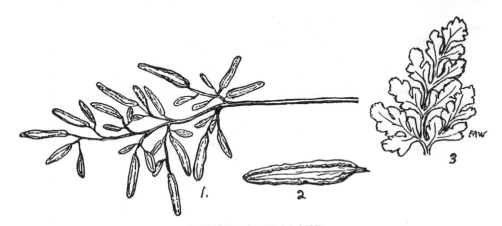

SLENDER CLIFF-BRAKE
(Cryptogramma Stelleri (S. G. Gmel.) Prantl)

Fertile frond shown is natural size. May be twice as long. Sterile frond has wider segments, as shown in Figure 3. The spores are under the rolled edges of the fertile frond, as shown in Figures 1 and 2. Usually grows on wet, limestone ledges. More common in central part of range at high altitudes.

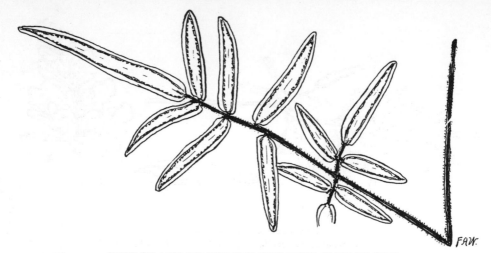

F.R.W.

CLIFF-BRAKE OR PURPLE-STEMMED CLIFF-BRAKE
(Pellaea atropurpurea (L.) Link)

Fronds 8—20 inches long; wiry; erect; tufted. Stipe and rachis covered by fine scales and purplish-brown. Lower pinnae sometimes single and sometimes three-parted. Grows in crevices of dry, limestone ledges. More common than the following species.

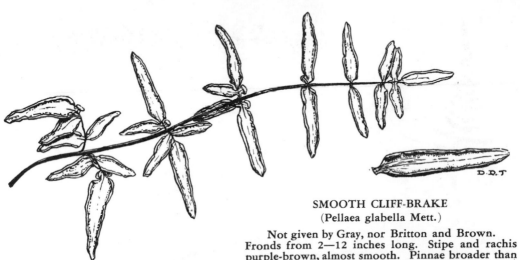

SMOOTH CLIFF-BRAKE
(Pellaea glabella Mett.)

Not given by Gray, nor Britton and Brown. Fronds from 2—12 inches long. Stipe and rachis purple-brown, almost smooth. Pinnae broader than Purple-stemmed Cliff-brake. Grows on dry, limestone ledges. Less common in this range than the Purple-stemmed Cliff-brake, but more common westward.

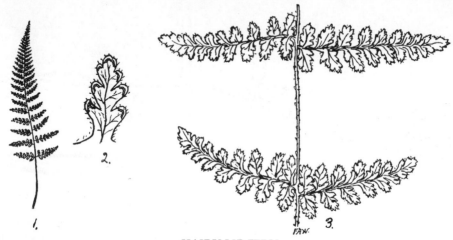

HAIRY LIP-FERN
(Cheilanthes lanosa (Michx.) Watt)

Frond shown was 12½ inches long. This is about as large as they grow. Figure 1 shows the shape of the frond. Figure 2 shows the rolled edges covering the spore cases. Figure 3 shows the lower pinnae of a sterile frond. Stipe and rachis brown; wiry; and covered with jointed hairs. Grows in tufts, on ledges.

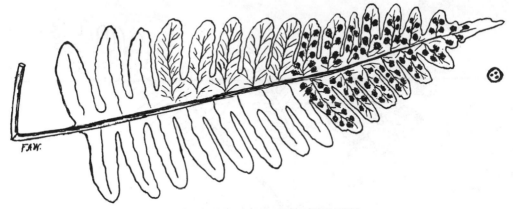

COMMON OR GOLDEN POLYPODY
(Polypodium virginianum L.), or (Polypodium vulgare L.)

Frond shown is natural size. Sometimes twice as long. Smooth and green throughout. Evergreen. Sori large, golden yellow when young, and without indusia. Sometimes confused with small fronds of the Christmas fern, from which it can be distinguished by the fact that the Polypody is not cut all the way to the midvein. Grows on rocky, moss-covered ledges. Common.

The green stipe is round at the base and the blade extends down the stipe at the top. Vascular bundles outlined in brown.

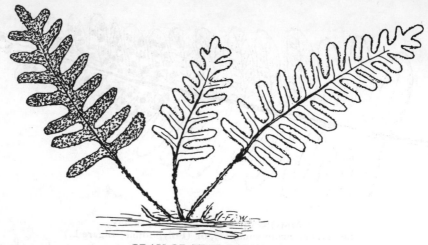

GRAY OR TREE POLYPODY
(Polypodium polypodioides (L.) A. S. Hitchc.)

Fronds shown are natural size. May be a foot long. Evergreen. Covered beneath with brown scales, attached by the center, which almost conceal the sori. Almost smooth above. Grows more commonly on the trunks of trees, but may be found growing on the ground. In forests of Pennsylvania and southward.

KEY BASED ON CHARACTERISTICS OF STERILE FRONDS

A. Blade entire
  B. Blade oval—page 4
  B. Blade not oval
      C. Blade broad and blunt at apex—page 66
      C. Blade not broad and blunt at apex
          D. Grass-like—page 16
          D. Not grass-like—page 67

A. Blade not entire
          E. Blade only lobed (not cut to midvein)
              F. Shallow lobes—page 74 and small leaves of page 75
              F. Deeply lobed (pinnatifid)
                  G. Thick in texture
                      H. Scaly beneath—page 90
                      H. Not scaly beneath
                          I. Stipe round—page 5
                          I. Stipe not round—page 89
                  G. Not thick in texture
                          J. Blade broadest near base—page 19
                          J. Blade broadest near center—page 64

          E. Blade more than lobed
                  K. Once pinnate (cut to midvein)
                      L. Stipe and rachis dark brown or black throughout
                          M. Stipe and rachis black—page 69
                          M. Stipe and rachis purplish-brown throughout
                              N. Pinna with entire margins—page 86 and small fronds of page 87
                              N. Pinna with toothed margins
                                  O. Pinna with auricle next to the rachis—page 68
                                  O. Pinna almost round—page 70

L. Stipe and rachis not dark brown or black throughout (may be dark at base)
    P. Dark brown at base
        Q. Stipe and ⅔ of rachis brown—page 75
        Q. Stipe dark at base only—page 71

    P. Green throughout
        R. Pinna rounded—page 23
        R. Pinna not rounded
            S. With auricle next to rachis—page 31 and 32
            S. With no auricle next to rachis—page 77

K. More than once pinnate
        T. Three-parted and each part triangular
            U. Fleshy in texture
                V. Stipe round, margins finely cut—page 7
                V. Stipe round, margins not finely cut
                    W. Lower triangle long-stalked—page 8 and 82—83
                    W. Lower triangle not long-stalked—page 6

            U. Not fleshy in texture
                X. Stipe round—page 9
                X. Stipe not round
                    Y. Thin in texture—page 38
                    Y. Thin in texture, palmately branched—page 84

        T. Not three-parted and each part triangular
                Z. Lowest pinna longest
                    aa. Stipe and rachis purple-brown throughout
                        bb. Free from scales—page 87
                        bb. With fine scales—page 88
                    aa. Stipe and rachis not purple-brown throughout

cc. Stipe dark brown at base or to blade only
    dd. Stipe dark brown at base—page 73
    dd. Stipe dark brown to blade—page 71

cc. Stipe not dark brown at base
    ee. Blade very narrow in proportion to length—page 23

    ee. Blade not very narrow in proportion to length
        ff. Divisions entire—page 85
        ff. Divisions not entire
            gg. Blade almost equilateral triangular—page 37
            gg. Blade not equilateral triangular—page 27

Z. Lowest pinna not the longest
        hh. Fronds shaped like a feather (branch evenly on each side)
           ii. Blade tapers to point at base
              jj. Blade broadest above center—page 21
              jj. Blade broadest about center—page 39

           ii. Blade not tapering to point at base
              kk. Lower pinna elongate-triangular or wedge-shaped
                ll. First lower pinnule next to the rachis, longest
                  mm. Blade broad in proportion to length—page 57
                  mm. Blade narrow in proportion to length—page 55

                ll. First lower pinnule not the longest
                  nn. Blade broadest at base
                    oo. Wiry in texture—page 88
                    oo. Not wiry in texture—page 29

                  nn. Blade not broadest at base
                    pp. Lower pinna triangular
                      qq. Free from scales—page 25
                      qq. Not free from scales

  rr. Blade scaly beneath—page 22
  rr. Scales on stipe and rachis only—page 45

 pp. Lower pinna elongate-triangular
   ss. Without spines on the margins—page 53
   ss. With spines on the margins
    tt. The second pinnule from the rachis longest—page 59
    tt. The second pinnule from the rachis not the longest
     uu. Texture thick—page 46
     uu. Texture not thick—page 48

kk. Lower pinna not elongate-triangular or wedge-shaped
    vv. No scales or hairs on stipe and rachis
     ww. Blade twice pinnate—page 11
     ww. Blade not twice pinnate
      xx. Veinlets joined forming chain along mid-vein—page 63
      xx. Veinlets not joined
       yy. Veinlets forked throughout blade—page 41
       yy. Veinlets not forked throughout blade
        zz. Thin in texture—page 43
        zz. Not thin in texture
         aaa. A tuft of down at base of each pinna—page 15
         aaa. No tuft of down at base of each pinna—page 13

    vv. Scales or hairs on stipe or rachis
        bbb. Stipe and rachis glandular hairy—page 79
        bbb. Stipe and rachis not glandular hairy

ccc. Black centered scales on stipe—page 81
ccc. No black centered scales on stipe
    ddd. Stipe covered with matted wool when young
        eee. Pinna and pinnules pointed—page 15
        eee. Pinna and pinnules rounded—page 13

    ddd. Stipe not covered with matted wool when young
        fff. Thickly covered on stipe and rachis with scales
            ggg. Pinnules bristle-tipped and winged—page 30
            ggg. Pinnules not bristle-tipped or winged—page 61

        fff. Thinly covered on stipe, rachis and sometimes veins with scales
            hhh. Blade elongate, triangular—page 35
            hhh. Blade not elongate-triangular
                iii. Lower pinna broadest in center—page 51
                iii. Lower pinna broadest next to the stipe—page 24

hh. Fronds not shaped like a feather, variously cut
                jjj. Blade palmately branched—page 84
                jjj. Blade not palmately branched
                    kkk. Climbing—page 17
                    kkk. Not climbing—page 72

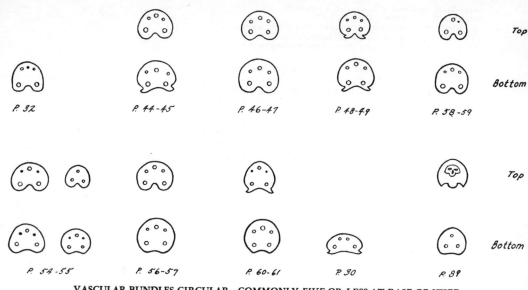

Top   Bottom

P. 32.   P. 44-45.   P. 46-47.   P. 48-49.   P. 58-59.

P. 54-55.   P. 56-57.   P. 60-61.   P. 30.   P. 89.

VASCULAR BUNDLES CIRCULAR—COMMONLY *FIVE* OR *LESS* AT BASE OF STIPE

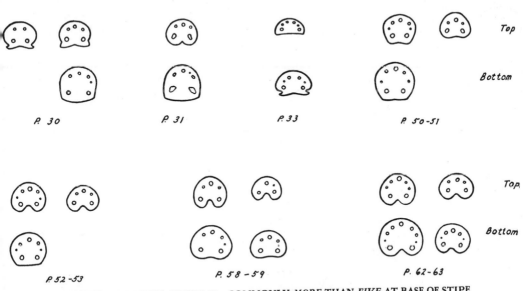

P. 30	P. 31	P. 33	P. 50-51

P. 52-53	P. 58-59	P. 62-63

VASCULAR BUNDLES CIRCULAR—COMMONLY *MORE* THAN *FIVE* AT BASE OF STIPE

Top

Bottom

P. 18-19   P. 22   P. 24   P. 28-29   P 39

Top

Bottom

P. 40-41   P. 42   P 64-65   P 76-77   P. 84

VASCULAR BUNDLES UNITED AT TOP OF STIPE

P. 6 P. 9 P. 10-11 P. 12-13 P. 14-15

Top

Bottom

P. 20-21 P. 36-37 P. 78-79 P. 80-81

Top

Bottom

VASCULAR BUNDLES FORM *HOOKED CURVES*

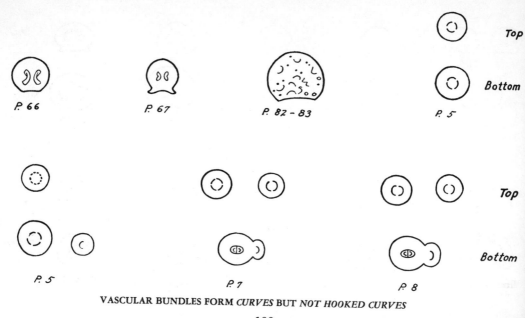

Top

Bottom

P. 66   P. 67   P. 82 – 83   P. 5

Top

Bottom

P. 5   P. 7   P. 8

VASCULAR BUNDLES FORM *CURVES* BUT *NOT HOOKED CURVES*

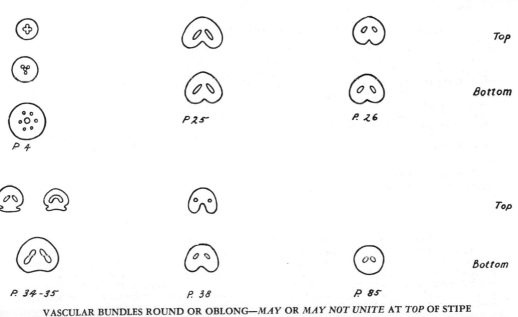

Top

Bottom

P. 25

P. 26

P 4

Top

Bottom

P. 34-35

P. 38

P. 85

VASCULAR BUNDLES ROUND OR OBLONG—*MAY* OR *MAY NOT UNITE* AT *TOP* OF STIPE

101

HOW TO COLLECT AND PRESERVE FERN SPECIMENS

If you wish to preserve fern specimens for a herbarium, try the following method:

Collect mature, normal-sized specimens and keep them moist until they are placed in a press. Place the fronds singly between layers of newspaper that equal the thickness of the stipe. If the frond is too large for the regulation sized mounting sheet (11½ x 17 inches) bend it over at about the center of the blade. Pile the fronds and layers of paper one on top of the other on the floor. Cap the pile with a board, equal in size of the paper, and a weight of rocks, or books, sufficiently heavy to keep the fern specimens from wrinkling while they dry. The newspaper should be changed every day until the ferns are dry. In good drying weather they should be ready to mount in about ten days. Attach the dry frond to a mounting sheet of paper by means of *narrow* strips of gummed paper placed at intervals across the stipe and rachis.

The name of the fern, its habitat, the date and place collected should be entered on the right, lower corner, of the mounting sheet.

HOW TO OBSERVE THE LIFE CYCLE OF A FERN

To observe the life cycle of a fern try the following procedure:

Collect spores from the Royal Fern when the spore cases have split open but are still slightly green in color. Dust the spores from the capsule-like spore cases onto a crumpled piece of blotter. Place the blotter in a dish containing a small amount of water (blotter must not be submerged), to insure a constant supply of moisture. Cover the dish with a glass and place in a light, warm place, but not in direct sunlight. The transformation from spore to thallus and then to the first tiny frond should take place in about three weeks.

GLOSSARY

Antheridium (ia)—The male organ of reproduction.

Archegonium—The female organ of reproduction.

Auricled—With one lobe at base.

Blade—The flat expanded part of a frond.

Clustered—Collected into a bunch.

Compound—Composed of two or more parts forming a whole.

Entire—Not toothed.

Fertile—Bearing spores.

Fronds—The leaves of ferns.

Gland—A secreting cell or group of cells.

Hairy—Beset with hairs.

Habitat—Locality in which plant grows.

Imbricated—Regularly overlapping.

Indusium (ia)—The covering for immature sori.

Midrib—The extension of the stipe through an undivided blade.

Midvein—See midrib.

Pinna (ae)—A primary division of a frond.

Pinnate—Blade cut to rachis.

Pinnate twice—Blade cut to rachis, and pinnae to midvein.

Pinnule—A division of a pinna.

Pinnatifid—Deeply cut but not cut to midrib.

Prothallium (ia)—The sexual stage of a fern.

Rachis—The extension of the stipe through the blade.

Scales—The chaff on stems of ferns.

Segment—One of the smaller divisions of a frond.

Sorus (i)—A group of sporangia.

Sporangium (ia)—The case in which spores develop.

Spore—A minute reproductive body, in ferns single-celled.

Sporophyte—The fern plant which bears the spores.

Spore Case—Pouch containing spores—same as Sporangium.

Spore Sac—Pouch containing spores.

Stalk—Same as stipe.

Stalked—With a stem.

Sterile—Without spores.

Stipe—The stem of a frond.

Tuft—A clump.

Vascular—Relating to ducts or vessels.

Veinlet—One of the small branches of the veins of a frond.

INDEX

106